I'm Dreaming You're Alive

Real Life True Romantic Story of Love, Loss & Friendship

CAT PHOTO BOOK

Copyright © 2020 Phil Epifano

All rights reserved.

ISBN: 979-8-6771-8645-5

This book is dedicated to my cat Ruby.

CONTENTS

1. Romance — 1
2. Intimacy — 8
3. Partnership — 14
4. Love — 21
5. He died — 32
6. Life Goes On — 33

ROMANCE

I'M DREAMING YOU'RE ALIVE

They had a great summer romance

The chemistry was instant

I'M DREAMING YOU'RE ALIVE

They talked for hours

I'M DREAMING YOU'RE ALIVE

He tells her that he loves her

I'M DREAMING YOU'RE ALIVE

Romantic love is a leisured experience

I'M DREAMING YOU'RE ALIVE

She wakes up and tells him that she loves him

INTIMACY

Sometimes, you need a hug

Sometimes, you need tough love

Here's the house where he lived

Being able to see each other every day is great

The moment every girl is dreaming of

Wearing a wedding dress

They embrace and talk

They're able to find some happiness

He was willing to carry her in his arms every day

PARTNERSHIP

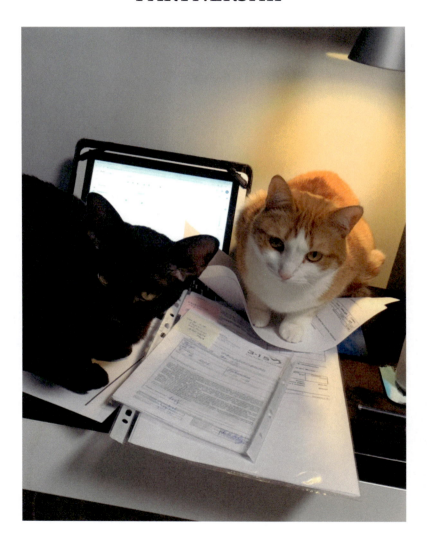

I'M DREAMING YOU'RE ALIVE

They can enjoy their mutual hobbies

They can enjoy home life

I'M DREAMING YOU'RE ALIVE

That evening they have dinner together

The relationship with a life partner is easy

Life is easier together

It's nice to be able to support each other when we have tough weeks

I'M DREAMING YOU'RE ALIVE

They're able to share everyday moments that come with living together

LOVE

I'M DREAMING YOU'RE ALIVE

Love is delicate

Love is one of the most fulfilling things

Love is real

Love grows with each passing day

I'M DREAMING YOU'RE ALIVE

Love conquers all

Love is a powerful emotion

Their love was strong

I'M DREAMING YOU'RE ALIVE

She proved herself to be a faithful friend

At a loss for words

I'M DREAMING YOU'RE ALIVE

Soulmates do not need words

He falls fatally ill

HE DIED

LIFE GOES ON

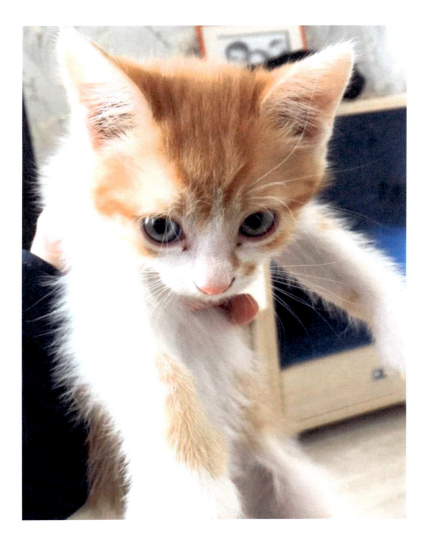

I'M DREAMING YOU'RE ALIVE

Very, very simple, very truly

I'M DREAMING YOU'RE ALIVE

I'm dreaming you're alive

Made in the USA
Columbia, SC
14 April 2025